Five-Six-Henry

Faithful to the End

Written by Gene Jordan

Illustrated by Kate Gehring

Published in the United States by CreateSpace

ISBN-13: 978-1503039407
ISBN-10: 1503039404
BISAC: Juvenile Nonfiction / Adventure & Adventurers

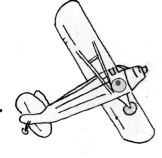

A note from the author

N5156H was the small Mission Aviation Fellowship Piper airplane flown by Nate Saint for what was called "Operation Auca," the effort to reach the "Auca" tribe (properly known as the Waodani) with the Good News of the Gospel.

This book is intended to retell a well-known story to a younger audience, through the eyes of the airplane. Every other page contains a hidden, descriptive word to allow for further discussion with your child. Our world, and especially the world of Five-Six-Henry, is a world of wonder, excitement, opportunity, and purpose. I retold this story to challenge a child, even at a very young age, to consider that God will use him or her for His purpose, if He is so permitted.

This story is completely documented in the books *Jungle Pilot, the Life and Witness of Nate Saint*, by Russell T. Hitt; and *Through Gates of Splendor*, by Elizabeth Elliot. It is also told in a children's video produced by The Voice of the Martyrs, *The Jim Elliot Story*. A movie adaptation of this story, *End of the Spear*, was released in 2005, with "Five-Six-Henry" as the star.

Parents might find it helpful to read some of these books and watch the movie, to be able to answer any questions that might follow the reading of this story.

Gene

Written for Canaan, Eden, Jordan, and Rajah, the most special grandchildren in the whole world! I hope that one day each of you will be used of God in a very special way.

Five-Six-Henry was built in a small airplane factory out in the country,

where the trees and fields stretched for miles.

The little airplane was especially proud the day they finished painting him a bright, shiny yellow.

His full name was November Five-One-Five-Six-Henry, but everyone just called him Five-Six-Henry. He couldn't wait to learn to fly!

After a final check at the factory to make sure everything was working right,

Five-Six-Henry took off for the very first time!

He loved practicing his flying maneuvers. He flew over the clouds and under the clouds. He tipped his wings to give a wave to the farmers and cows below.

What could be better than gliding with the birds? The earth below seemed peaceful and quiet as he gazed at his surroundings.

Excitement

Five-Six-Henry practiced extra hard at learning to land precisely where he wanted to touch down. He knew someday he might have to land at a very short airstrip.

One day a tall, blond man showed up at the airplane factory. He seemed excited to meet Five Six Henry.

Five-Six-Henry could tell he was about to have a new owner!

Sure enough, the very next day Five-Six-Henry took off with his new owner at the controls.

He waved a quick goodbye to his friends at the factory, and that day he flew longer than he had ever flown before.

He skimmed high over mountains.

**He pushed his way through pounding rain and skirted
around a lot of clouds. He flew low along the ocean shore.**

Five-Six-Henry was tired when he finally bounced down on a very small airstrip at the edge of a large rainforest.

After a good overnight sleep, Five-Six-Henry was eager to discover what his new life would be like.

His pilot and passengers were men and women who loved Jesus. People called them missionaries.

Five-Six-Henry soon found out that flying over the jungle was the happiest part of his day.

One of Five-Six-Henry's most favorite flights was when he was able to carry a small child out of the jungle and take him to the hospital for help.

After missionary doctors and nurses helped the child get better, Five-Six-Henry would happily fly the healthy boy or girl back to the child's jungle village.

Early one morning, Five-Six-Henry heard the pilot and his friends talking about a group of people who lived deep in the jungle. They had never heard about Jesus. "Who will tell them that Jesus loves them? They don't like strangers and they don't trust anyone," said the pilot.

Preparation

Five-Six-Henry began making flights over this village and dropping gifts to the people below. Shiny pots, fish hooks, and colorful ribbons fell by parachute. Five-Six-Henry wanted them to know that he was a very friendly airplane.

One day Five-Six-Henry spotted a very small sandbar on the edge of a winding river, not too far from the village where they dropped the gifts. "I could land there," he thought.

That night, while he rested in his airplane hangar, Five-Six-Henry dreamed about the sandbar. He knew he could land there, even though it might be tricky. He practiced landing over and over in his mind.

Five-Six-Henry made several trips with supplies back and forth to the beach. He got really good at landing on the tiny sandbar.

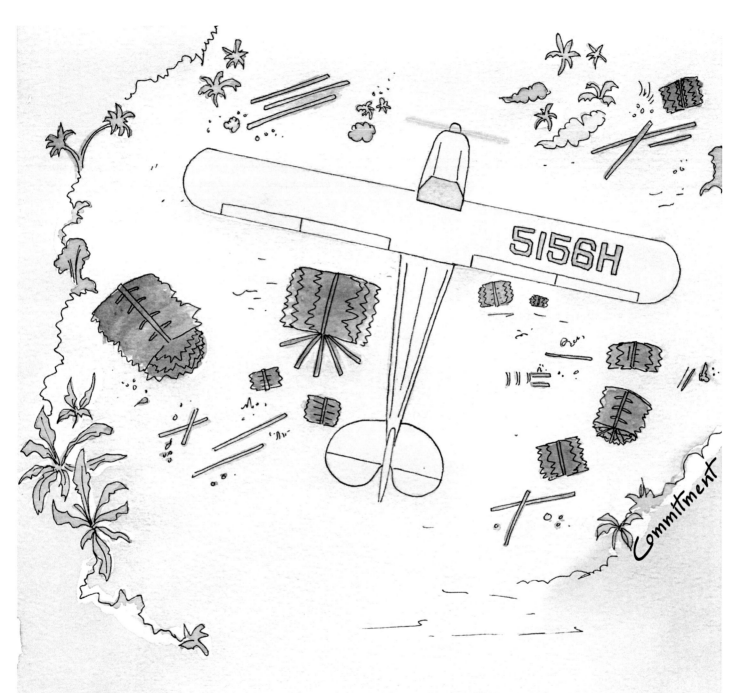

Sometimes, on the way to the beach, he would fly over the nearest jungle village. His passenger would shout out to the people below, "We are your friends! Come to the beach!"

One afternoon, while Five-Six-Henry was resting on the sand bar, three native people suddenly appeared out of the thick forest of trees. They went right over to look curiously inside Five-Six-Henry.

The missionary men were very glad to have visitors. They tried hard to explain that they wanted to be friends but, since they couldn't speak their language, they just gave them big smiles.

But... the natives didn't understand the missionaries' message. They were afraid of the strange men and their large wooden bird. So they did something very sad.

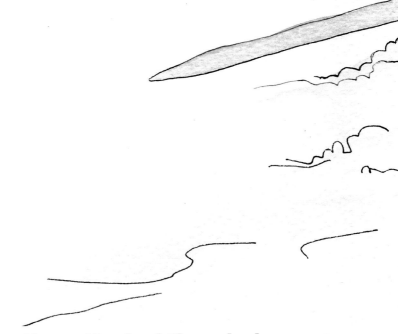

With their sharp spears they attacked the missionary men and killed them.

Then they turned their anger on Five-Six-Henry! They hit him with machetes and stuck their spears right through him.

They cut his bright yellow covering and damaged his wings and tail so that he could never fly again!

Five-Six-Henry sat crumpled on the beach with a broken heart. He knew he was really good at landing on the beach, but now he would never fly over the jungle again.

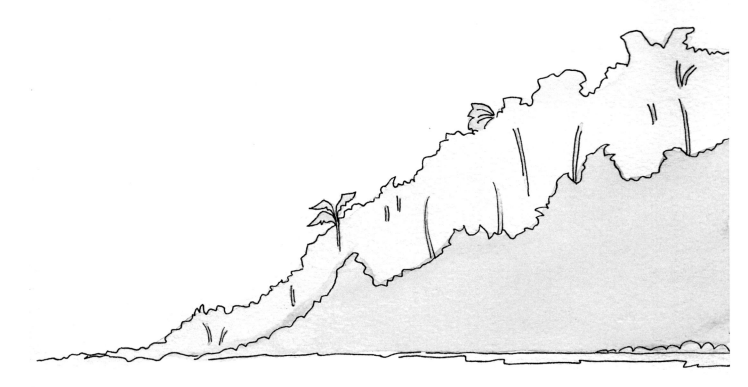

He really wanted to be a part of telling these people how much Jesus loved them. But now...his flying days were over. God's job for Five-Six-Henry was done.

After the natives left, Five-Six-Henry thought about his service to others. How he loved helping people by flying them quickly over the jungle!

How he especially enjoyed taking patients to the hospital where they could get help!

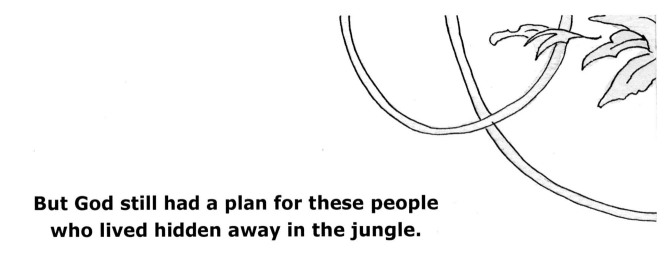

But God still had a plan for these people
who lived hidden away in the jungle.

Personal Responsibility

A few years after the missionary men were killed, the pilot's sister and one of the missionary men's wives walked over a long and muddy jungle trail until they reached the village.

They learned to speak their language and taught them to read.

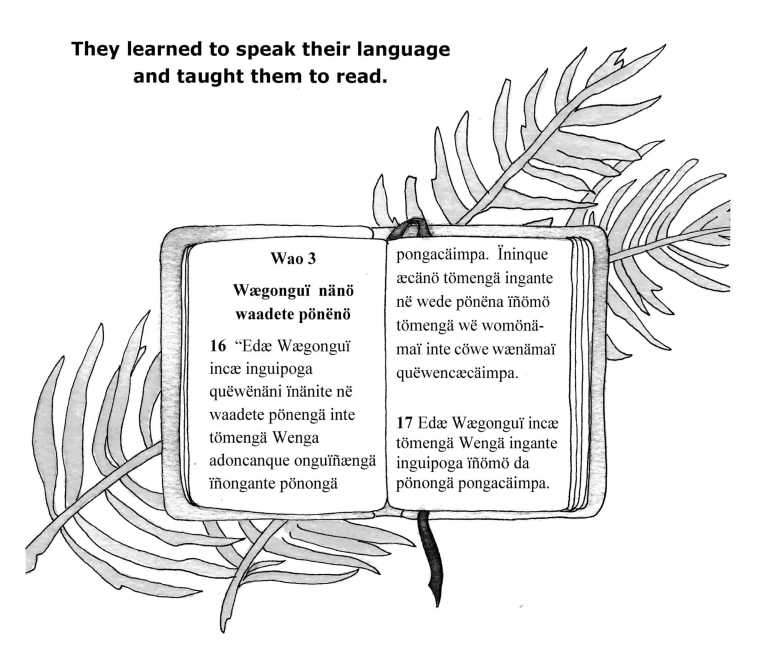

Wao 3

Wægonguï nänö waadete pönënö

16 "Edæ Wægonguï incæ inguipoga quëwënäni ïnänite në waadete pönengä inte tömengä Wenga adoncanque onguïñængä iñongante pönongä pongacäimpa. Ïninque æcänö tömengä ingante në wede pönëna ïñömö tömengä wë womönämaï inte cöwe wænämaï quëwencæcäimpa.

17 Edæ Wægonguï incæ tömengä Wengä ingante inguipoga ïñömö da pönongä pongacäimpa.

Today some of the Waodani follow Jesus with all their heart and are even telling other people in their tribe about Jesus.

**Five-Six-Henry was a faithful airplane; he had
done everything his pilot asked him to do.**

Will you be faithful, just as Five-Six-Henry was faithful, and do what God asks you to do?

Today, what is left of Five-Six-Henry stands proudly in a small display at MAF's headquarters in Idaho.

All of the boys and girls who come to visit him hear of his adventures in the jungle.

But most importantly, they hear about a jungle tribe

who finally heard the message of Jesus' love.

Gene and pilot Nate Saint

Gene grew up in Ecuador and actually flew in Five-Six-Henry as a small boy.

He later returned to Shell, Ecuador with Mission Aviation Fellowship and worked as a pilot for twenty-two years in the Amazon jungle where Five-Six-Henry flew.

Kate graduated from Seattle Pacific University with an emphasis in art. As a teenager, she spent five years living in Central Asia with her family. She now lives in British Columbia with her husband.

Five-Six-Henry is her first illustrated children's book.